The State of Food Insecurity in Manzini, Swaziland

Daniel Tevera, Nomcebo Simelane, Graciana Peter and Abul Salam

Series Editor: Prof. Jonathan Crush

ACKNOWLEDGEMENTS

The findings on urban food security in Manzini reported in this paper are based on data from the 2008–2009 AFSUN Urban Food Security Household Survey. We wish to thank the Canadian International Development Agency (CIDA) for funding the study through the UPCD Tier One Program, the eight geography students at the University of Swaziland who administered the survey, the Deputy Prime Minister of Swaziland and his office, and the Ministers of Housing and Urban Development, Education, and Agriculture and Cooperatives, for participating in the national dissemination workshop that was co-hosted by the University of Swaziland and the Municipality of Manzini. We would also like to thank Professor Jonathan Crush for his input and suggestions. Finally, we wish to acknowledge the people of Moneni, Ticancweni and Standini who provided the information on which this paper is based.

AFSUN

© AFSUN 2012

Published by the African Food Security Urban Network (AFSUN)
African Centre for Cities, University of Cape Town, Private Bag X3
Rondebosch 7701, South Africa; and
Southern African Research Centre, Queen's University,
152 Albert Street, Kingston, ON K7L 3N6, Canada
www.afsun.org

First published 2012

ISBN 978-1-920597-05-4

Cover photograph: AP Photo/Siphiwe Sibeko

Production by Bronwen Müller, Cape Town

AUTHORS

Daniel Tevera is Professor in the Department of Geography, Environmental Science and Planning, University of Swaziland.

Nomcebo Simelane is Head of the Department of Geography, Environmental Science and Planning, University of Swaziland.

Graciana Peter is a Senior Lecturer in the Department of Geography, Environmental Science and Planning, University of Swaziland.

Abul Salam is a Senior Lecturer in the Department of Geography, Environmental Science and Planning, University of Swaziland.

Previous Publications in the AFSUN Series

CONTENTS

TABLES

FIGURES

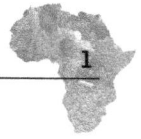

1. INTRODUCTION

Swaziland is one of Africa's smallest countries with a total area of 17,360km^2 and a population of just over 1 million, mostly subsistence farmers on communal Swazi Nation Land. Although the country is often viewed as rural, no one lives far from an urban centre and most rural households have members living in town or in the urban areas of neighbouring South Africa. An estimated 25% of the population resides in urban areas, a number projected to grow to nearly 40% by 2030.[1] The stagnation of the country's economy in recent years has led to an increase in poverty, high unemployment (over 30%) and income inequality.[2] About 45% of Swaziland's population lives in extreme poverty, subsisting on less than USD1 per day.[3] Female-headed households are the poorest and tend to be larger in size than other households. Despite more than a decade of government policies that have as their goal to reduce poverty and gender-based inequalities, women and children continue to be poorer and more disadvantaged than other groups, both in monetary terms and in having their basic needs met.

Over the last decade, Swaziland has also been devastated by the HIV and AIDS pandemic. The country's HIV prevalence rate is now among the highest in the world.[4] UNAIDS estimated in 2010 that HIV prevalence was 26% and that 184,000 people were living with HIV.[5] Prevalence is higher among women than men.[6] People living in urban areas (34% HIV positive) are at significantly higher risk of infection than those in rural areas (at 24%). HIV prevalence among urban women aged between 15 and 49 years is 37% (compared to 29% of rural women of the same age). For men in the same age bracket, the figures are 26% (urban) and 17% (rural).[7] HIV is not significantly correlated with income, with similar prevalence rates in all income groups. Prevalence is much higher among the employed than the unemployed (32% versus 18%).[8]

The negative socio-economic impacts of HIV and AIDS in Swaziland have been examined in previous studies.[9] So, too, have the implications of the epidemic for household food security, although the primary focus has been on rural household agricultural production.[10] The UN's Food and Agriculture Organization (FAO) and World Food Programme (WFP) argue that HIV and AIDS in Swaziland is "the main underlying driver of food insecurity at the household level. It affects households by limiting their ability to generate income and cultivate by increasing the number of people that need to be taken care of, and taking the lives of the traditional caregivers. It impacts on the assets of households, affects the policies, institutions and processes that influence livelihoods and forces adaptations to livelihood strategies."[11]

Swaziland as a whole is extremely food insecure and, since the early 1990s, has shifted from being a net exporter of food to depending on food aid to feed its population. During the 2007 drought, for example, 650,000 people in Swaziland received emergency food aid from outside the country. In 2008, the FAO estimated that about 210,000 people nationwide were food insecure, 150,000 chronically so.[12] Total cereal utilization for the year April 2008 to March 2009 was an estimated 212,000 tonnes against domestic production of around 75,500 tonnes, with the shortfall met by importing from South Africa and food aid.[13]

Assessments of food insecurity in Swaziland have tended to focus on rural areas and producers.[14] The 2006 Swaziland Vulnerability Assessment interviewed 996 rural Swazi households across the country and grouped them into four main types: food insecure (21% of total), food assistance beneficiaries (26%), moderate to good food access (35%) and best access to food (18%). In other words, a total of 47% of households were either food insecure or insecure enough to be receiving food aid.[15] All four administrative regions of Swaziland were classified as having low acute malnutrition (<5%) but significant medium (10-29%) to high (30-39%) chronic malnutrition prevalence.[16] Two-thirds of households reported experiencing environmental and economic "shocks" in the previous year which had interfered with their ability to eat, live and retain assets.[17] Around 40% of households changed their diets in response to these shocks and 40% engaged in disbursement of assets. The 2006 study unfortunately did not consider the food security situation of urban households.

The 2006–2007 Swaziland Demographic and Health Survey researched both rural and urban households and found that the former were generally in a more precarious situation. For example, the survey found that 29% of children under the age of 5 suffered from stunted growth (43% of those aged 18-23 months) and that stunting was more common among rural than urban children (30% versus 23%).[18] The survey also showed that the proportion of adults who were too thin or malnourished is relatively low (6% of women and 21% of men) especially when compared with the number who are overweight or obese (51% of women and 18% of men). Overnutrition increases with age in both men and women in Swaziland (39% of men and 76% of women aged 40-49 are overweight or obese) but urban men are markedly healthier than their rural counterparts (with lower rates of under- and overnutrition). However, urban and rural women have similar rates of undernutrition and overnutrition (56% of urban women are overweight or obese but so are 49% of rural women).[19]

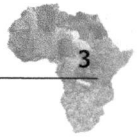

Studies of urban food security include a 2008 survey by the Swaziland Vulnerability Assessment Committee (Swazi VAC) and WFP and a follow-up 2010 study by the Food Economy Group.[20] The Swazi VAC study interviewed 450 households in four urban areas (Manzini, Mbabane, Nhlangano and Siteki) and concluded that only 4% of households had "poor" food consumption, 10% had "borderline" food consumption, 23% had "acceptable" consumption and 64% had "good" food consumption in terms of dietary diversity and food frequency.[21] The study also identified five food security groups: food insecure (21% of households), food secure but poor with no stress (33%), food secure with high stress (15%), food secure (24%) and highly food secure (7%).[22] Of the areas examined, Manzini was found to have the least overall food insecurity, "where it is assumed people have better access to a variety of foods due to higher purchasing power."[23] This study affords the opportunity to revisit and compare these findings about urban food insecurity in Swaziland in the light of an in-depth study of Manzini.

2. METHODOLOGY

Manzini is Swaziland's commercial hub and second largest city, after the capital Mbabane. The city has experienced considerable in-migration during the past 20 years and the Greater Manzini urban and peri-urban area (which includes the industrial area of Matsapha) now has a population close to 100,000. Rapid urbanization through rural-urban migration and natural population growth has led to the growth of many unplanned settlements with low-quality housing, poor sanitation, unhealthy living conditions, high levels of poverty and a shortage of job opportunities.[24] The AFSUN Food Security Baseline Survey, of which this study is part, focused on acquiring a regional picture of food insecurity in poor urban neighbourhoods across the SADC region. Consequently, this report focuses on poorer, low-income areas of the city. Where appropriate, the findings are compared with those of the 2006 Swazi VAC urban study for Manzini.

Three low-income suburban areas of the city were surveyed for the project: Moneni, Ticancweni and Standini (Figure 1). Moneni is in the eastern part of Manzini, 4km from the city centre. Ticancweni is a newer informal settlement that has been incorporated into the city, while Standini is an older suburb that has been impoverished for many years. The survey was implemented in December 2008 by eight final-year geography students at the University of Swaziland under faculty supervision. Household data from the Manzini City Council provided a sampling frame which was used to determine the number of respondents to interview in the three study areas. Systematic sampling was used to select 500 households for interview (Table 1). These households contained a total population of 2,112 people. The average household size was 4.2 and the largest household contained 20 people. The study was conducted in consultation with the Manzini City Council which informed the local leadership structures prior to the survey.

FIGURE 1: Location of Study Areas

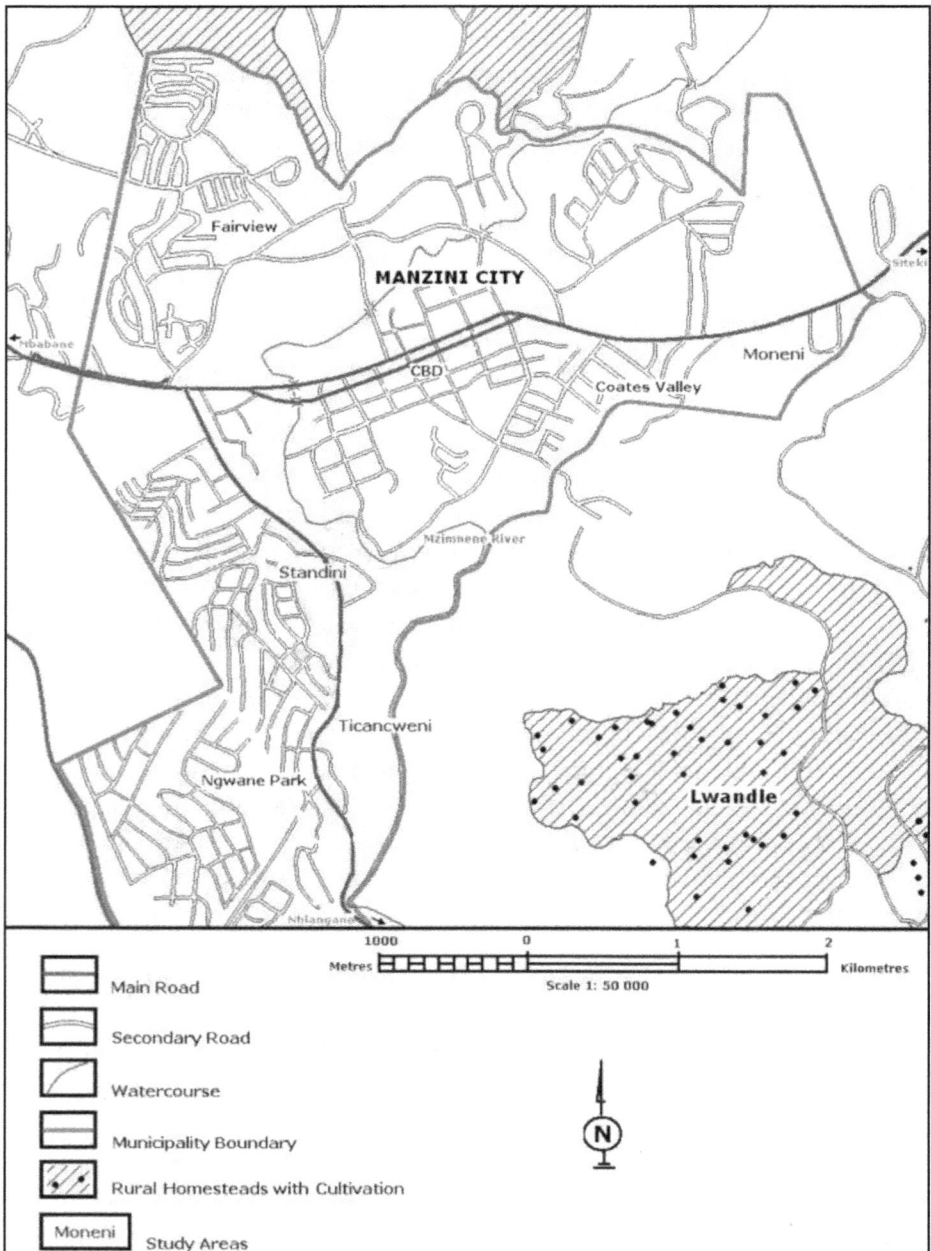

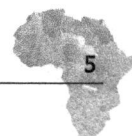

TABLE 1: Population and Sample Size				
Study area	Population (2007)	No. of households	Sample size	% of households sampled
Moneni	3,729	1,071	250	23.4
Ticancweni	1,374	390	150	38.5
Standini	660	201	100	49.8
Source: Swaziland Population and Housing Census, 2007				

Female-centred households (with a female head and no male spouse or partner) made up nearly 40% of the total sample. Next were male-headed nuclear households at just under one-third. The proportion of male-centred households (households without a female spouse or partner) was much lower, at 18%. The proportion of extended-family households was only 13%, in sharp contrast to Swaziland's rural areas where they are particularly common. Urban households in Swaziland tend to be smaller than their rural counterparts. The 2006-2007 Health and Demographic Survey, for example, found that 86% of urban households had between 1 and 5 members compared with 57% of rural households.[25] The mean size of households was 3.0 in urban areas and 5.4 in rural areas. This survey found that 75% of poor households in Manzini had between 1 and 5 members and 21% had between 6 and 10 members (Table 2). This suggests that households tend to be larger in the poorer parts of cities like Manzini.

TABLE 2: Household Characteristics		
Household structure	No.	%
Female-centred	189	38.7
Male-centred	86	17.6
Nuclear	152	31.1
Extended	61	12.5
Child-headed	1	0.2
Total	489	100.0
Household size	No.	%
1–5	369	75.5
6–10	103	21.1
>10	17	3.5
Total	489	100.0
N=489		

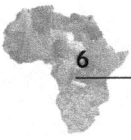

3. SOURCES OF FOOD FOR POOR URBAN HOUSEHOLDS

3.1 Sources of Purchased Food

At the local level, food security depends on the capacity of individuals and households to produce their own food or buy and use food of sufficient quantity and quality through all seasons. Understanding the different strategies households use to access resources and promote food security is therefore essential. Where do low-income households in Manzini get their food from? The survey found that households purchase the bulk of their food and that producing food for their own consumption is not an important source at all. Clearly, access to food is being met largely through formal food channels at a time when the purchasing power of the poor is shrinking.

South African supermarkets have made major inroads into the Swaziland food supply system and several big South African companies (Spar, Shop-rite and Pick n Pay) have food retail outlets in Manzini.[26] In addition, there are a number of smaller, locally-owned supermarkets. The importance of supermarkets as a source of food purchase for the poor of Manzini was very evident from the survey (with 92% of households stating that they normally obtain food from this source) (Figure 2). Much less important for bought food were the informal food economy (regularly patronised by 48% of households) and smaller outlets such as grocers, butchers and fast-food outlets (patronised by 46%).

The informal food economy brings together artisanal food producers involved in the production, preparation and provision of relatively cheap food for consumers of particular class and income configurations. Groups of food processors and vendors are very heterogeneous and include poor women selling small amounts of cooked food on the streets and small, medium and micro enterprises (SMMEs) processing, distributing and selling large quantities of both processed and unprocessed foods. Informal market/street food is an important source that brings together rural farmers, urban growers and other food producers who choose to sell their produce directly to consumers. The needs of low-income households and informal food traders and the context in which exchange takes place frequently give rise to the formation of an informal economy in which agro-food networks flourish.

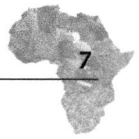

Many food vendors buy uncooked food from the main food market in Central Manzini and from nearby farms and sell cooked food on the streets. Despite the fact that "street food" is generally cheaper than super-market food, as noted above, less than half of the households surveyed normally buy food from informal vendors and only 38% had done so in the previous week. A possible explanation was offered in two separate studies of Manzini which noted that the incentives for participation in the informal economy are limited by municipal prohibitions on street vend-ing, harassment by the police, tight control over the distribution of stalls at the city marketplace and high levels of competition.[27]

FIGURE 2: Sources of Purchased Food for Poor Households

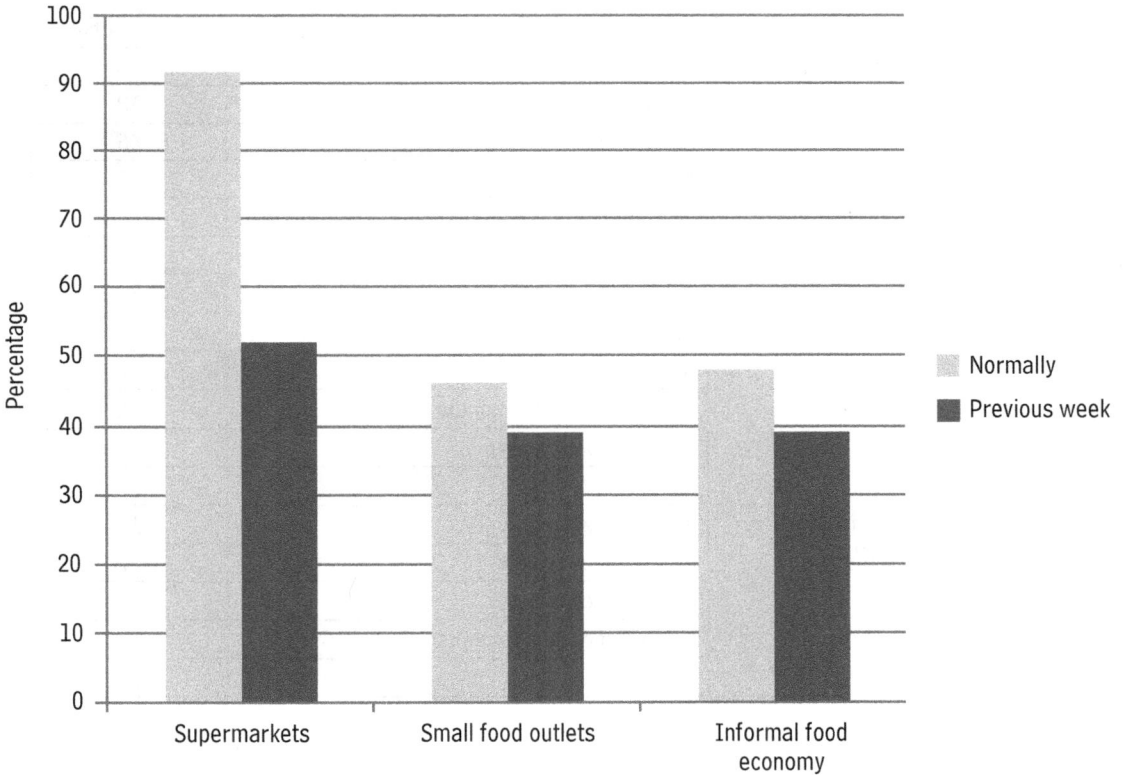

3.2 Frequency of Patronage

Only half of the households (52%) had bought food at supermarkets in the week prior to the survey (Figure 2). This suggests that while super-market food reaches almost all households on a regular basis, they do not shop there every day or even every week. Analysis of the frequency of use of the three main food sources indicates very different patterns of patron-

age (Table 3). Only 5% of households shop at supermarkets almost every day, compared with 10% for the informal food economy and 13% for small outlets. Twenty-three percent of supermarket patrons shop at least once a week, compared with 37% of informal economy users and 39% of small-outlet shoppers. There are several possible reasons for the higher frequency of purchases from informal and smaller retail outlets including the tendency to buy small quantities of perishables such as vegetables, meat, bread and milk, as well as cooked food. The majority of households that buy from supermarkets confine their purchases to once a month (65%), probably soon after payday, so that they can take advantage of the savings obtained from buying in bulk.

TABLE 3: Frequency of Food Purchase by Food Source		
		% of households
Supermarkets	At least five days a week	5
	At least once a week	18
	At least once a month	65
	At least once in six months	1
	Less than once a year	1
	Never	10
Small outlets	At least five days a week	13
	At least once a week	26
	At least once a month	7
	At least once in six months	<1
	Less than once a year	<1
	Never	53
Informal food economy	At least five days a week	10
	At least once a week	27
	At least once a month	7
	At least once in six months	1
	Never	55

3.3 Food Purchase by Type and Size of Household

As might be expected, the importance of various food sources differs somewhat according to household structure (Table 4). All categories of household indicated that their top three food sources were supermarkets, small outlets and the informal food economy. The most significant difference is between extended-family households and the others: extended-family households rely less on food purchase from all three sources, but especially supermarkets, than households in the other three categories.

TABLE 4: Normal Sources of Purchased Food by Household Type				
	Female-centred (% of households)	Male-centred (% of households)	Nuclear (% of households)	Extended (% of households)
Supermarkets	93	92	95	80
Small food outlets	46	50	54	51
Informal food economy	50	50	47	44
N	189	86	152	61

The hypothesis that household size matters in shaping food purchasing strategies finds some support in the data (Table 5). Smaller households (with 1-5 members) are slightly more likely to patronize supermarkets than larger households. They are also less likely to buy food from small outlets and street vendors than households in the 6-10 member range. However, very large households with more than 10 members (of which there are too few to generalize) patronize all three sources less frequently. Their use of small outlets and informal sources is significantly lower.

TABLE 5: Normal Sources of Purchased Food by Household Size			
	1–5 (% of households)	6–10 (% of households)	>10 (% of households)
Supermarkets	93	87	88
Small food outlets	45	50	24
Informal food economy	47	53	36
N	369	103	17

When food sourcing is analyzed on the basis of household income, the three main purchase sources remain dominant. However, it is clear that levels of household income have an impact on supermarket patronage (Table 6). The better off the household (even in poorer communities such as these) the more likely it is to purchase food from supermarkets. The supermarket is clearly the leading food source for almost all households in the upper income tercile (97% compared with 79% in the lowest tercile). Supermarkets sell food in bulk, which works well for better-off households because this means their food is cheaper per unit. The very poor are unable to buy food to put aside for a week or two because they lack storage facilities and tend to live from hand to mouth.

TABLE 6: Normal Sources of Purchased Food by Household Income			
	Poorest (SZL<600) (% of households)	Less poor (SZL600–SZL1,299) (% of households)	Least poor (>=SZL1,300) (% of households)
Supermarkets	79	92	97
Small food outlets	55	52	49
Informal food economy	55	54	47
N	100	131	117
SZL1 (Swazi Lilangeni) = ZAR1 (South African Rand) = USD0.11			

3.4 The Practice of Urban Agriculture

AFSUN has taken issue with the conventional wisdom that urban agriculture is the most likely means of ensuring food security for poor urban households, arguing that its importance has been greatly exaggerated.[28] This is certainly the case in the study areas in Manzini where urban agriculture, involving the growing of vegetables and maize by households and the keeping of livestock, is not an important food source. Only 10% of households surveyed produce any of their own food through urban agriculture (and only 4% had consumed home-grown produce in the week prior to the survey).

In Swaziland urban agriculture is a precarious activity that remains technically illegal despite its supposed benefits for household food security and nutrition. Municipal by-laws state explicitly that farming is prohibited in urban areas. Despite the fact that authorities do not use heavy-handed tactics to discourage the activity, very few urban households in Swaziland engage in off-plot urban agriculture. Those that do generally do not own the land but use public space or vacant lots of private owners, with or without their permission. However, the amount of available land has declined considerably in recent years with the conversion of vacant and agricultural land to housing.[29]

Although the vast majority of surveyed households of all types (90%) do not participate in urban agriculture, some household characteristics make participation more likely. For example, extended-family households are most likely to participate in urban agriculture (16% of households), followed by female-centred households (11%). Very few male-centred or male-headed nuclear households (less than 5% of each) are involved in urban agriculture. While some might see this as an indication that urban agriculture is the preserve of poorer households and undertaken by some women as a survival strategy, the findings show that it is the better-off households that are more likely to be involved in urban agriculture than

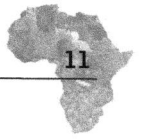

their poorer counterparts. Some 6% of households in the lowest-income tercile and 4% in the middle-income tercile produce some of their own food. However, 12% of households in the upper-income tercile engage in urban agriculture. This suggests that the relationship between food poverty and urban agriculture is not a simple one, although the actual numbers that produce their own food are so small that it is difficult to be definitive. Larger households are also more likely to engage in urban agriculture than smaller ones although, again, the relationship is not simple: 20% of households with 6–10 members cultivate some of their own food compared with only 12% of larger households (>10 members) and 7% of smaller households (1–5 members).

3.5 Intra-Urban Food Sharing

Various forms of community and intra-household food sharing are an important food source for a significant minority of poor households in Manzini. For example, almost one in five households (19%) said that borrowing food was normal for them, and 11% had done so in the week before the survey (Figure 3). Eighteen percent normally obtain food from charitable food kitchens and 13% had done so in the previous week. Again, 18% said it was normal to be given food by neighbours and relatives in the community (and 10% had obtained food this way in the previous week). Far less important as normal sources of food are food remittances, food aid and sharing meals with other households, although 6% had shared meals in the previous week. In another question, household heads were asked if they had received food from relatives or friends in other cities over the course of the previous year: 7% had received food from relatives and 9% from friends.

An analysis of food sharing by household type reveals some interesting differences (Table 7). Extended-family households are clearly most reliant on these food sources, with 26% regularly borrowing food and 24% obtaining food from community kitchens. The contrast between female-centred and male-centred households in the use of community food kitchens is stark (21% versus 3%). On the other hand, male-centred households are equally likely as female-centred households to borrow food and slightly more likely both to obtain food from other households and to share meals with them.

FIGURE 3: Sources of Shared Food

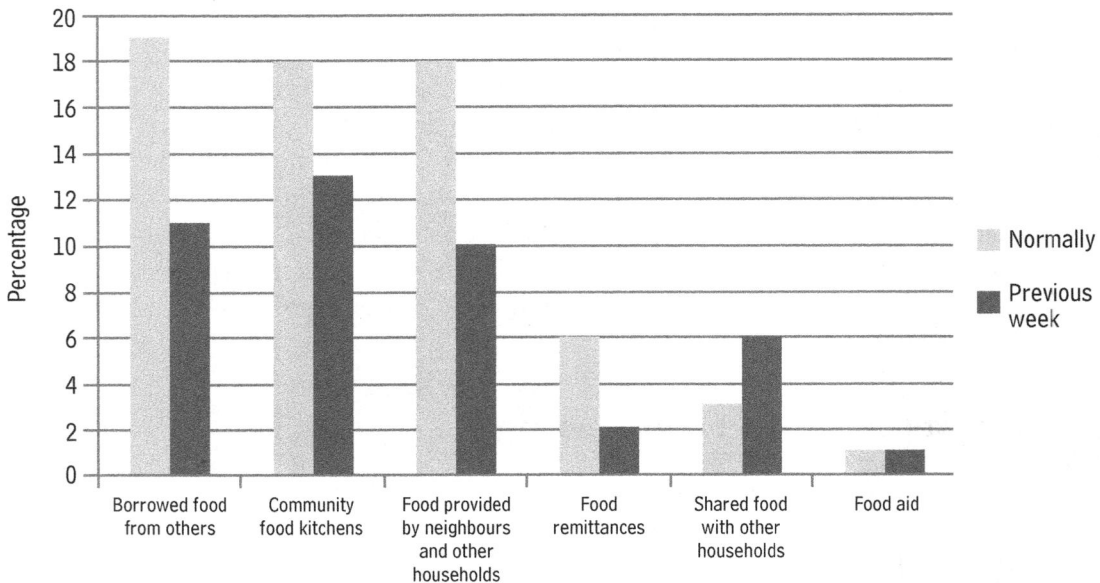

TABLE 7: Sources of Shared Food and Household Type				
	Female-centred (% of households)	Male-centred (% of households)	Nuclear (% of households)	Extended (% of households)
Community food kitchens	21	3	18	24
Borrowed food from others	18	19	16	26
Food provided by neighbours and other households	13	16	9	18
Shared food with other households	7	13	7	10
Food remittances	5	7	0	2
Food aid	1	0	1	0
N	189	86	152	61

Since extended-family households are likely to be larger than other types of household, it might reasonably be expected that there would also be a relationship between household size and use of shared food. In fact, the differences are relatively small between households with less and more than 5 members, with one marked exception (Table 8). One-third of households in the larger group normally obtain food from community kitchens, compared with only 11% of those in the smaller group. In other words, increasing household size seems to lead to greater reliance on non-monetary sources of food. One of the likely reasons is that larger, extended-family households have less disposable income to spend on food.

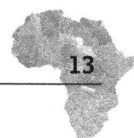

TABLE 8: Sources of Shared Food and Household Size		
	1–5 (% of households)	6–10 (% of households)
Borrowed food from others	18	21
Food provided by neighbours and other households	14	13
Food remittances	13	4
Community food kitchens	13	33
Food aid	–	2
Shared food with other households	4	5
N	369	103

Finally, as might be expected, the usage of non–purchased food sources is closely tied to income levels (Table 9). Community food kitchens are used by 29% of households in the lowest-income tercile but only 15% in the upper-income tercile. Similarly, food provision by neighbours and other households is clearly related to income (20% in the lower tercile, 12% in the upper tercile). For reasons that are unclear, however, households in the lowest- and highest-income tercile are equally likely to borrow food (23-24%) whereas those in the middle-tercile are far more likely to do so than either of the other groups (35%). These households are also more likely to share meals with others.

TABLE 9: Sources of Shared Food and Household Income			
	Poorest (<SZL600) (% of households)	Less poor (SZL600–SZL1,299) (% of households)	Least poor (>=SZL1,300) (% of households)
Community food kitchens	29	22	15
Borrowed food from others	24	35	23
Food provided by neighbours and other households	20	15	12
Shared food with other households	13	21	4
Food remittances	4	3	7
Food aid	1	–	1
N	100	131	117

3.6 Rural-Urban Food Transfers

An aspect of urban food security that has often been ignored is the informal transfer of food from families in the rural areas.[30] As noted above, few poor households in Manzini grow any of their own food and yet there is

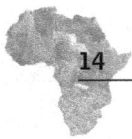

a definite seasonal pattern to food shortages in the city. In part, this may be related to the fact that urban households are partially dependent on food transfers, and therefore on the surpluses and shortages of the rural agricultural cycle. Across the eleven cities in the AFSUN survey, just over a quarter of households (28%) had received food from relatives and/or friends in the rural areas in the previous year. In some cities (including Windhoek, Lusaka and Harare) the proportion was over 40% (Figure 4). Manzini is in the next cluster of cities with just over a third receiving food transfers (a group that includes Maseru and Blantyre).

FIGURE 4: Food Transfers to Urban Households

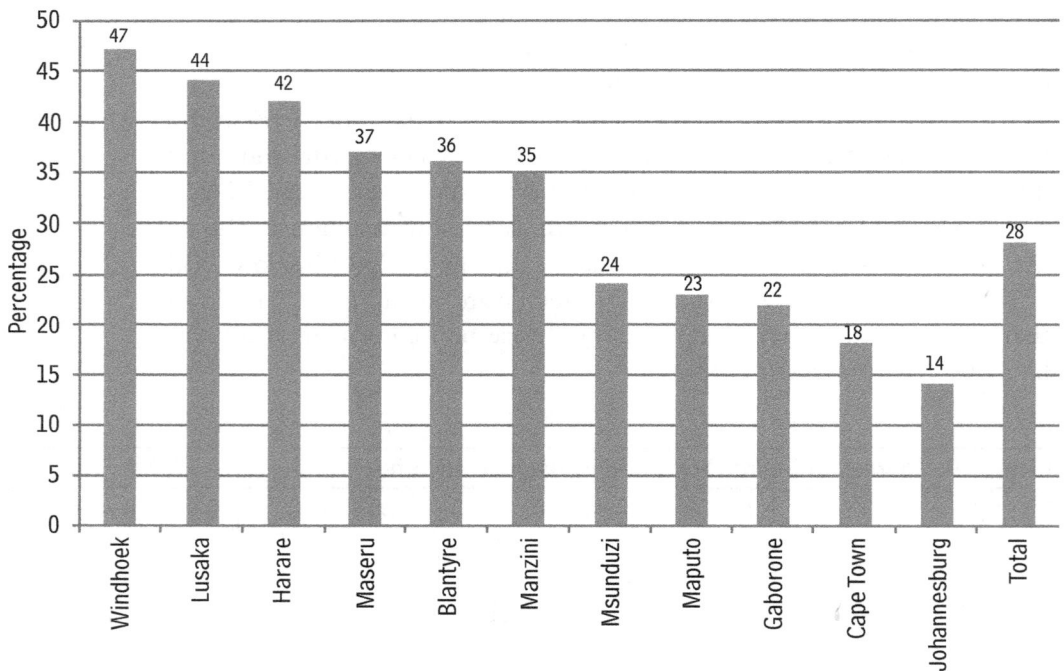

Most of the food obtained from the rural areas consists of cereals (primarily maize). Twenty-two percent of all households and two-thirds of recipient households receive cereals. Other foodstuffs – including vegetables, fruit, meat or poultry – are received by less than 10% of households overall. One-third of the 7% of households getting food from rural areas receive vegetables. Indigenous vegetables are relatively common in the rural areas to supplement household diets but storage and processing problems may inhibit transfer to relatives in town.[31] Only 6% of households receiving food transfers said they were critical to household survival. However, 86% said they were important/very important to the household.

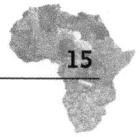

TABLE 10: Types of Foods Received from Rural Areas		
	% of total households	% of recipient households
Cereals	22	66
Vegetables	7	31
Sugar or honey	4	18
Roots or tubers	3	11
Meat or poultry or offal	3	14
Foods made with oil, fat, or butter	3	11
Beans, peas, lentils, or nuts	2	9
Fruit	1	5
Cheese, yoghurt, milk or other milk products	<1	3
Eggs	<1	2
N	452	108

4. LEVELS OF FOOD INSECURITY IN POOR URBAN HOUSEHOLDS

4.1 Levels of Household Food Insecurity

This section attempts to answer the following questions: what are the levels of household food insecurity in the poor areas of Manzini? What are the main characteristics of food insecure households? How does gender affect household food security? Are there temporal dimensions to household food insecurity? The AFSUN baseline survey, of which the Manzini study is part, used four measures designed to capture the access dimensions of food insecurity: the Household Food Insecurity Access Scale (HFIAS), Household Food Insecurity Access Prevalence Indicator (HFIAP), Household Dietary Diversity Scale (HDDS) and the Months of Adequate Household Provisioning Indicator (MAHFP):

HFIAS: This score is a continuous measure of the degree of food insecurity in the household in the month prior to the survey.[32] An HFIAS score is calculated for each household based on answers to nine "frequency-of-occurrence" questions. The minimum score is 0 and the maximum is 27. The higher the score, the more food insecurity (access) the household experienced. The lower the score, the less food insecurity (access) the household experienced.

HFIAP: This indicator categorizes households into four levels of household food insecurity: food secure, and mild, moderately and severely

food insecure.[33] Households are categorized as increasingly food insecure as they respond affirmatively to more severe conditions and/or
experience those conditions more frequently.

HDDS: Dietary diversity refers to how many food groups are consumed
within the household over a given period.[34] The maximum number,
based on the FAO classification of food groups for Africa, is 12. An
increase in the average number of different food groups consumed
provides a quantifiable measure of improved household food access.
In general, any increase in dietary diversity reflects an improvement in
the household's diet.

MAHFP: This indicator captures changes in the household's ability to
ensure that food is available above a minimum level all year round.[35]
Households are asked to identify in which months (during the past
12 months) they did not have access to sufficient food to meet their
household needs.

The average HFIAS score for Manzini was 14.86. Manzini's mean HFIAS
was the highest of all eleven cities surveyed (Table 11). Only Harare had
a comparably high score and that city was in the midst of the worst economic crisis in its history at the time of the survey.[36] What this means, in
effect, is that Manzini's poor households have the highest levels of food
insecurity in the entire regional study. The survey found that only 18%
of households had always had enough food in the previous year. Thirty-
three percent had gone without sufficient food several times while the rest
(49%) had gone without many times or always.

TABLE 11: Manzini HFIAS Compared to Other Cities			
	Mean	Median	No.
Manzini, Swaziland	14.9	14.7	489
Harare, Zimbabwe	14.7	16.0	454
Maseru, Lesotho	12.8	13.0	795
Lusaka, Zambia	11.5	11.0	386
Msunduzi, South Africa	11.3	11.0	548
Gaborone, Botswana	10.8	11.0	391
Cape Town, South Africa	10.7	11.0	1,026
Maputo, Mozambique	10.4	10.0	389
Windhoek, Namibia	9.3	9.0	436
Blantyre, Malawi	5.3	3.7	431
Johannesburg, South Africa	4.7	1.5	976

On the HFIAP scale, over three-quarters of the surveyed households in Manzini were severely food insecure (79%), with very few moderately food insecure (12%) and mildly food insecure (2%) households. Only 6% of households were food secure (Figure 5). This was certainly not the lowest figure across the eleven surveyed cities. However, the proportion of severely food insecure households was higher in Manzini than in any other city (Table 12).

FIGURE 5: Household Food Insecurity Access Prevalence Scale

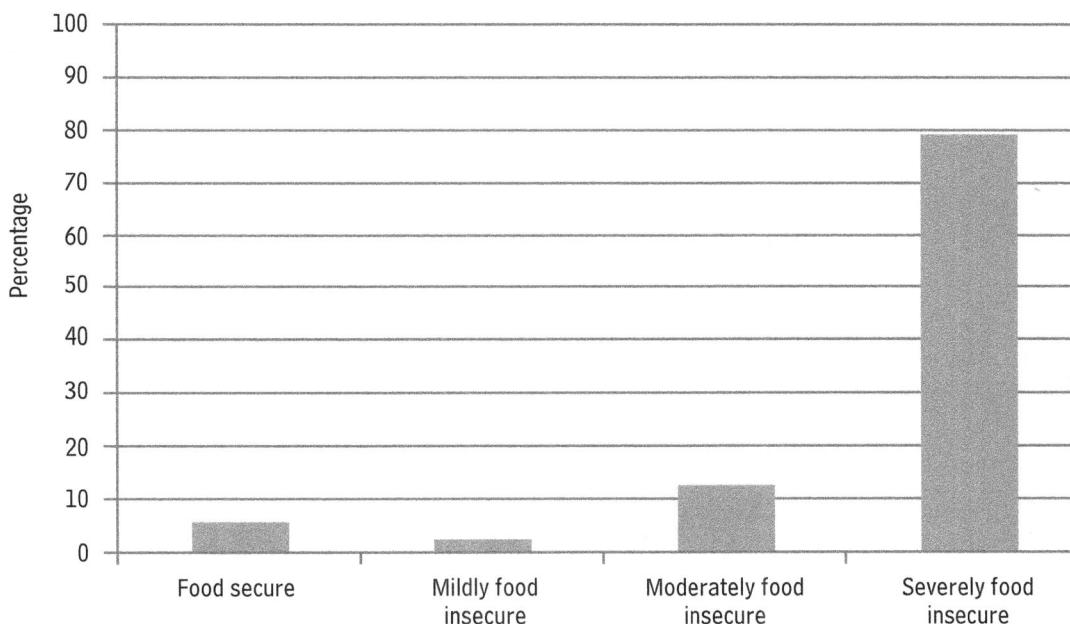

TABLE 12: Food Insecurity in Manzini Compared to Other Cities		
	Severely food insecure (% of households)	Food secure (% of households)
Manzini, Swaziland	79	6
Harare, Zimbabwe	72	2
Lusaka, Zambia	69	4
Cape Town, South Africa	68	15
Maseru, Lesotho	65	5
Windhoek, Namibia	63	18
Gaborone, Botswana	63	12
Msunduzi, South Africa	60	7
Maputo, Mozambique	54	5
Johannesburg, South Africa	27	44
Blantyre, Malawi	21	34

Household heads were asked a series of questions about their food situation in the month prior to the survey. Two-thirds of the household heads said they were sometimes or always worried that there would not be enough food in the household (Table 13). Half said there was sometimes or often no food at all to eat. Just over a quarter said that household members had gone to sleep hungry because there was not enough to eat. And one-quarter said they had gone without food for a whole day.

TABLE 13: Frequency of Hunger in the Household		
		%
Did you worry that your household would not have enough food?	No	16
	Rarely	17
	Sometimes	30
	Often	37
Was there ever no food to eat of any kind in your household because of lack of resources to get food?	No	27
	Rarely	24
	Sometimes	22
	Often	28
Did you or any household member go to sleep at night hungry because there was not enough food?	No	48
	Rarely	24
	Sometimes	17
	Often	11
Did you or any household member go a whole day and night without eating anything because there was not enough food?	No	56
	Rarely	20
	Sometimes	14
	Often	10

4.2 Dietary Diversity

The HDD score ranges from 0 (least diverse, where none of the types of food are eaten) to 12 (most diverse, where all food groups are eaten). The average HDD score for surveyed households was 4.07 which indicates that dietary diversity is low. Most households had eaten cereals (96%) and vegetables (60%) the previous day (Figure 6). Nearly half had eaten meat or poultry and sugar or honey. However, the proportion eating from other food groups was much lower.

FIGURE 6: Types of Food Eaten in Previous 24 Hours

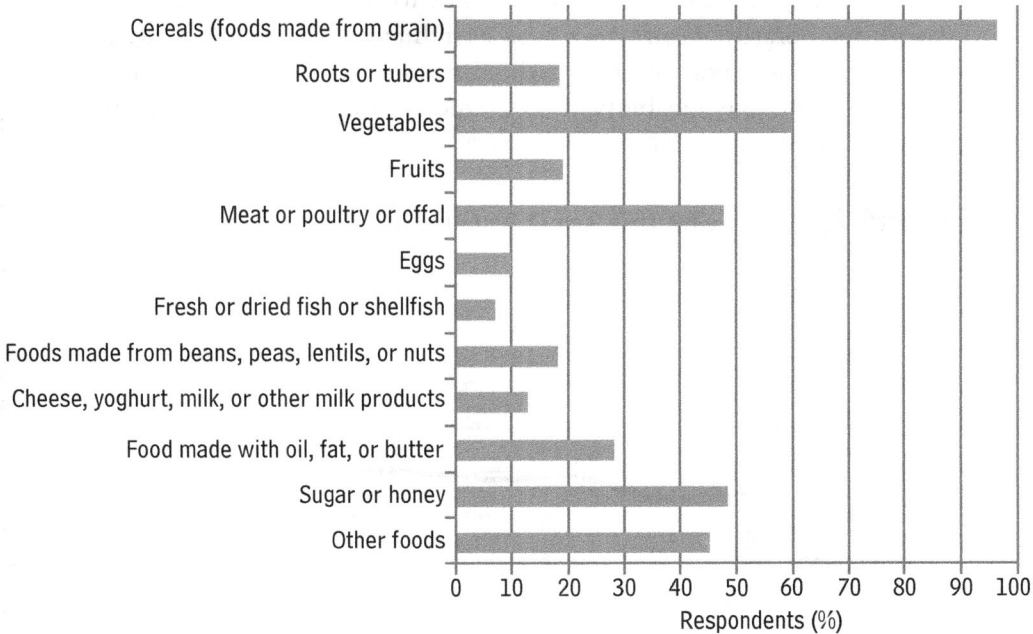

4.3 Seasonality and Food Insecurity

The MAHFP is incremental; as the score increases towards 12 (the maximum), so does the adequacy of food provisioning in the household. The survey found a mean score of 5.87 for the whole sample, while households classified as moderately and severely food insecure on the HFIAP scored even lower at 4.68. Both these scores are very low by absolute and regional standards and indicate that in Manzini there are only about 5–6 months (for the urban poor in general) and 4–5 months (for food-insecure households only) of adequate food provisioning.

April, May and December are more food secure, while January, February, March, September and October are the worst months for most households. In January, 75% of surveyed households did not have enough to eat, followed by February (67%), March (62%), October (61%) and September (60%) (Figure 7). Fewer households experienced inadequate food provisions in April (45%), May (46%) and December (43%). April and May coincide with the annual harvesting period which increases food availability in households and markets. By September supplies are drying up. In some years, December can benefit from additional harvests from the short rains (September to December in good seasons), as well as remittances from returning/visiting migrants from South Africa during the Christmas vacation period. Also, some employees receive extra income in December (13th cheque). The increased income tends to improve household food security temporarily. From January to March crops are not yet ready for harvest and a large portion of household income is likely to be spent on school fees. Also, the possibility of over-expenditure during the December festive season cannot be ruled out.

FIGURE 7: Months with Insufficient Food to Eat

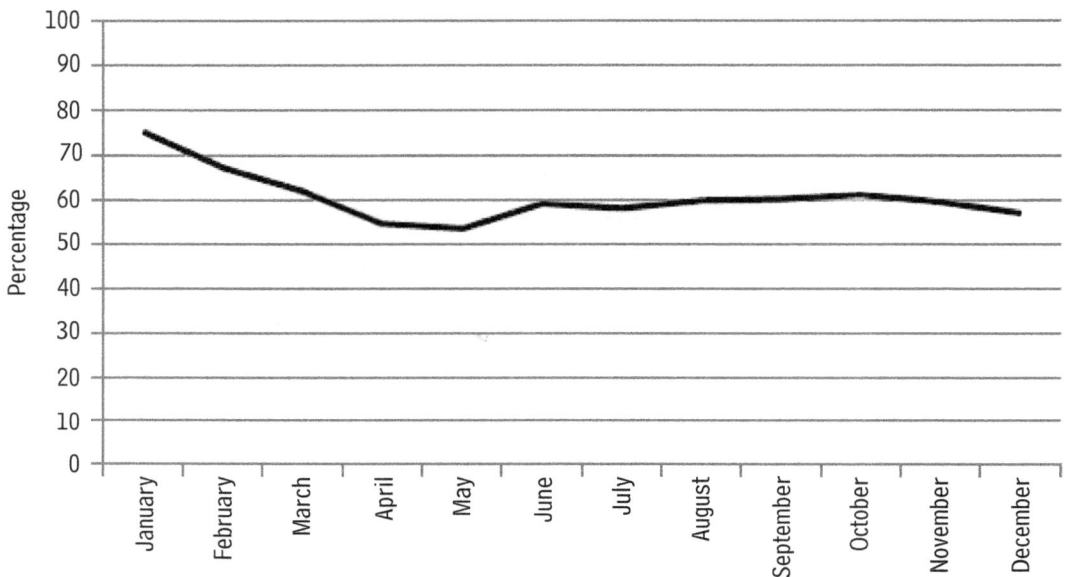

4.4 Common Responses to Food Insufficiency

When households cannot access enough food, they resort to a variety of coping strategies. Diets change, for example, and people eat food they do not like, but which may be more affordable. In the previous month, 71% of households had eaten food they did not want to because of a lack of resources (Table 14). Another response of the food insecure is to eat smaller meals and portions: 64% of households had done this in the previous month. Or again, households may be forced to reduce the number of meals they eat in a day: 57% of households had eaten fewer meals because there was insufficient food available. A total of 24% of households had sometimes gone without a cooked meal for a day during the previous week.

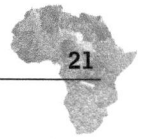

TABLE 14: Responses to Lack of Food Access		
		%
Did you or any household member have to eat some foods that you really did not want to eat because of a lack of resources to obtain other types of food?	No	10
	Rarely	20
	Sometimes	23
	Often	48
Total	100	
Did you or any household member have to eat a smaller meal than you felt you needed because there was not enough food?	No	17
	Rarely	19
	Sometimes	25
	Often	39
Total	100	
Did you or any household member have to eat fewer meals in a day because there was not enough food?	No	20
	Rarely	23
	Sometimes	21
	Often	36
Total	100	
Were you or any household member unable to eat preferred foods because of a lack of resources?	No	10
	Rarely	15
	Sometimes	31
	Often	44
Total	100	
Did you or any household member eat a cooked meal less than once a day?	No	34
	Rarely	24
	Sometimes	24
	Often	18
Total	100	

5. CAUSES OF EXTREME FOOD INSECURITY

As noted above, 79% of households in the survey were severely food insecure and 12% were moderately food insecure. Because food insecurity is so pervasive, we might reasonably assume that it is impossible to determine which households are more likely to be food insecure than others. This section examines whether there are any differences in food insecurity by such variables as household structure, household type and household income.

First, in terms of household structure there were slight differences. For example, although very few households in any category were food secure, the number was smallest among female-centred households (at 4%) (Table 15). Female-centred households also made up the greatest proportion of severely food insecure households (82%). Extended-family households were the lowest proportion of severely food insecure, possibly because they have a better chance of having more than one wage earner.

TABLE 15: Household Structure and Level of Food Insecurity				
	Male–centred (% of households)	Female–centred (% of households)	Nuclear (% of households)	Extended (% of households)
Food secure	6	4	8	7
Mildly insecure	0	3	3	2
Moderately insecure	13	11	13	16
Severely insecure	81	82	76	75
N=489				

Second, household size appears to have an impact on food insecurity. Again, the vast majority of all households are severely food insecure but it is clear that large households are the most food insecure. No household with more than 10 members was food secure, and 88% of this category was severely food insecure (Table 16). Mid-sized households (with 6–10 people) were marginally more food secure than their smaller counterparts.

TABLE 16: Household Size and Level of Food Insecurity			
	Household size		
	1–5 (%)	6–10 (%)	>10 (%)
Food secure	5	8	0
Mildly insecure	2	3	0
Moderately insecure	13	12	12
Severely insecure	79	78	88
N=489			

Third, because most households buy their food from retailers, do not produce any of their own food and do not have access to social welfare, household income is a critical determinant of food security. This is true even within the poorest urban communities. So, for example, 94% of households in the poorest-income tercile were severely food insecure, compared with 90% in the middle-income tercile and 66% in the higher-income tercile (Table 17). Similarly, the proportion of food-secure households was 1%, 2% and 15% respectively. Since the level of food insecurity is relatively similar in the lowest two terciles, it does appear that an income of more than SZL1,300 (USD150) per month represents something of a threshold in reducing the prevalence of food insecurity.

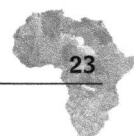

TABLE 17: Household Income Terciles by Level of Food Security			
	Household Income Terciles		
	Poorest (SZL<600)	Less poor (SZL600–SZL1,300)	Least poor (>=SZL1,300)
Food secure	1	2	15
Mildly insecure	0	2	3
Moderately insecure	5	6	16
Severely insecure	94	90	66
N=340			

Fourth, in the past decade Swaziland entered a prolonged period of economic stagnation and crisis.[37] The Swazi economy has one of the slowest growth rates in Africa and poverty and unemployment have reached record levels. To survive, many households are forced to rely on a diverse set of income-generating activities. These include wage employment, casual labour, informal marketing, manufacture and sale of crafts, rent, formal and informal loans, and begging. Two-thirds of households in the poor areas of urban Manzini with incomes of more than SZL1,300 per month (SZL15,600 or USD1,800 per annum) are severely food insecure and another 16% are moderately food insecure. According to the Swazi VAC, the main sources of income of all urban households in Swaziland are salary/wages (51%), small business (22%), cash crop production and sales (13%), remittances (13%) and petty trade (12%).[38] Dependence on salaries/wages was highest in Manzini (62%). This means that the availability of wage employment (and unemployment levels), the types of jobs and wages paid, and the availability and prices of foodstuffs are likely to have a major impact on household food security. At the most basic level, irrespective of actual incomes from each of these strategies, there is a clear relationship between food security and the number of strategies pursued by a household. The proportion of severely food insecure households drops from 83% of households with one strategy to 56% of households with four or more strategies. Similarly, the proportion of food secure and mildly insecure households increases from 4% to 22% (Table 18).

TABLE 18: Households Income Strategies by Level of Food Security				
	No. of strategies			
	One (% of households)	Two (% of households)	Three (% of households)	Four or more (% of households)
Food secure	3	4	7	15
Mildly insecure	1	4	7	7
Moderately insecure	13	12	7	22
Severely insecure	83	80	79	56
N=461				

Fifth, the purchasing power of households that do earn income has declined precipitously with general inflation and rising food prices. The hike in inflation levels after 2003 impacted negatively on low-income households that depend mainly on food purchase for consumption. The staple food in Swaziland is maize, which is sometimes substituted by rice and wheat products (bread and flour). Due to erratic weather patterns, staple food production has fallen short of meeting domestic consumption requirements over the past decade. National maize output was 67,639 tonnes in 2001-2002 but dropped to 26,170 tonnes in 2006-2007.[39] The price of maize meal has remained relatively steady because it is government-controlled. However, commodities such as cooking oil, rice, meat and chicken have shown steep increases in price. Bread has also seen drastic increases as wheat is imported and many low-income households find it difficult to buy bread on a regular basis. The price of cooking oil and rice increased by over 100% between June 2007 and April 2008. Cooking oil and rice are imported and are highly vulnerable to price changes as their price is affected by global markets and currency fluctuations. Local poultry farmers are said to be going out of business in the face of "unfair competition from imported and often dumped poultry products from other countries, such as South Africa."[40] Many poorer households prefer to buy live chickens from local suppliers, which are cheaper, but continued supply is far from assured.

Finally, there is the question of whether rural-urban links and food transfers reduce overall levels of food insecurity as they do, for example, in Windhoek.[41] The evidence from this survey suggests that they may make a small difference to some households but two-thirds of households receive nothing from the rural areas and the overall impact seems negligible. Consider, for example, those households who do receive food transfers: only 4% are food secure and 78% are severely food insecure. This compares with figures of 6% and 79% for the sample as a whole.

6. GENDER AND FOOD SECURITY

This section identifies gender differences in food access at the level of the household. Given the very high food insecurity for all households, any differences in levels of food insecurity would not be large. As noted above, the proportions of female-centred and male-centred households that were severely food insecure on the HFIAP scale were very similar (82% and 81%), as were the proportions that were food insecure (6% of male- and 4% of female-centred households).

Despite the similarities in levels of food insecurity, there are marked differences in household income. For example, 39% of female-centred households are in the lowest-income tercile compared to 29% of male-centred households (Figure 8). There are also fewer female-centred households in the upper-income tercile (24% versus 28%). The average income for a female-centred household was SZL1,064 (USD122) per month compared to SZL1,312 (USD150) per month for male-headed households. In other words, although female-centred households generally have lower incomes they are not significantly more food insecure than male-centred households.

FIGURE 8: Household Structure by Household Income Categories

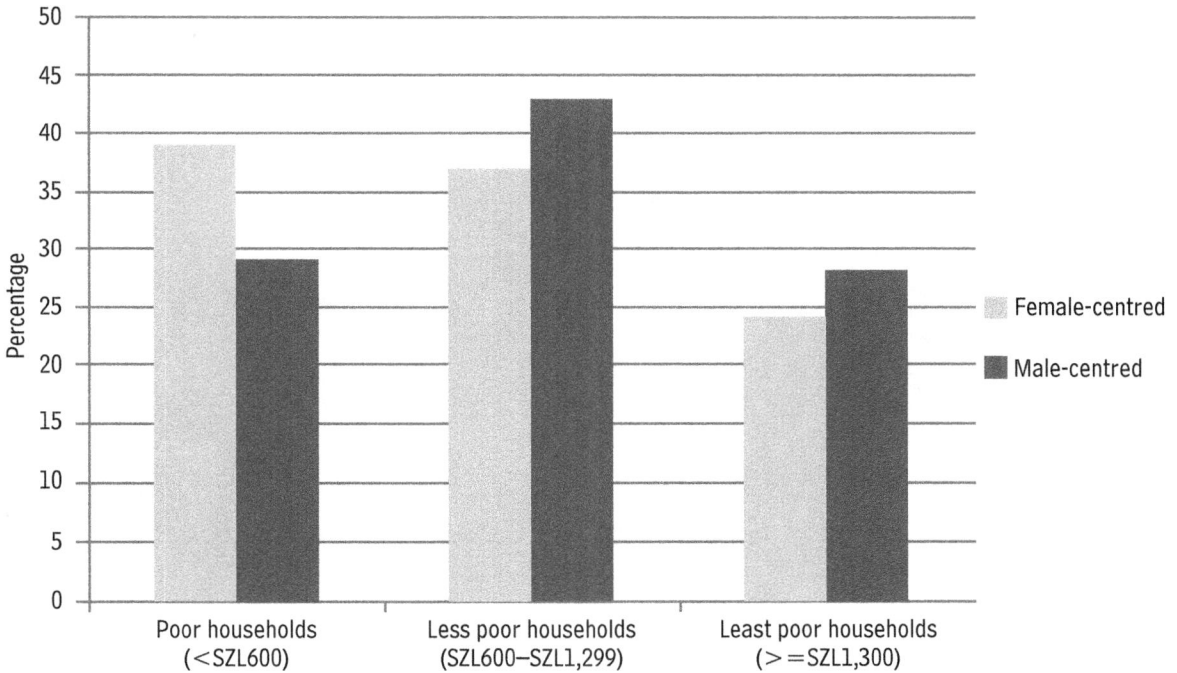

In part, the income differential is a function of gendered employment and income-generating strategies. Formal sector employment is virtually non-existent in the sample. Casual labour (both formal and informal) is the primary income source for both men and women but more men than women find employment (25% versus 20%) (Figure 9). Women are more likely than men to derive income from informal-marketing activity (16% versus 9%). Other income sources with clear differences include self-employment (more men than women) and renting space to lodgers (more women). More women make income from selling home produce but men find it easier to access formal and informal credit. In sum, female heads do not have the same access to important strategies such as casual labour and formal credit, and depend more on informal credit, marketing, rentals and gifts. These strategies are not only risky, cost more and have lower financial returns but also increase women's socio-economic vulnerability.

FIGURE 9: Sources of Household Income

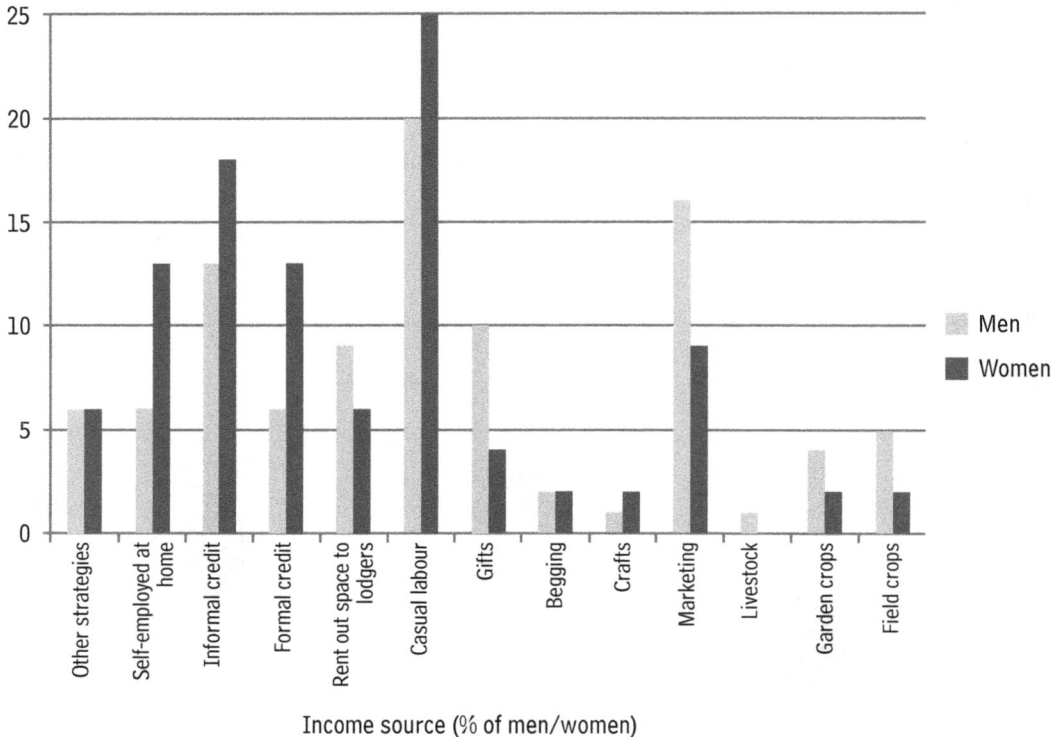

Income source (% of men/women)

7. CONCLUSIONS AND RECOMMENDATIONS

Recent assessments of food insecurity in Swaziland have focused predominantly on the rural areas largely because that is where about 75% of the population resides. However, studies done elsewhere in Africa show that urban food insecurity is intensifying and has become chronic. This study, which was part of the AFSUN baseline survey involving eleven cities in Southern Africa, provides information on the food security situation of

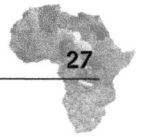

households in selected low-income areas of Manzini, the economic hub of Swaziland. The four measures used to capture the various dimensions of food insecurity reveal several important findings:

- Food insecurity in the low-income suburbs of Manzini is an acute problem that will increase because of high and volatile food prices fuelled by the global economic crisis and the increased frequency of weather shocks, especially drought. The findings reveal five groups comprising households that are food insecure (21% of households), food secure but poor with no stress (33%), food secure with high stress (15%), food secure (24%) and highly food secure (7%). The HFIAS score of 14.86 shows that many households are severely food insecure while the HDDS score value of just 4.09 is indicative of low levels of dietary diversity. Tables 11 and 12 show clearly that the urban poor of Manzini are less food secure than the poor in the other AFSUN project cities and this partly explains why city and national policy-makers in Swaziland should be concerned about urban food security challenges facing the country.

- Poverty is a key factor behind the high food-insecurity levels among the poor in Manzini, but the relationship between the two is complex as not all poor households are food insecure. Also worth noting is that households which are severely food insecure tend to be very large (with more than 10 members), female-headed and female-centred, and have a narrow range of livelihood strategies.

- Urban household food insecurity has a temporal dimension, with January, February, March, September and October as the severe hunger months for the majority of households.

- The supermarket is the leading food source for almost all households in the upper-income tercile (97% compared with 79% in the lowest tercile). The fact that the majority of low-income urban households in Manzini purchase most of the food that they consume presents numerous problems because their irregular and low incomes are inadequate to pay for other basic needs such as housing, health, transport and education.

- Very few households get their food from food aid, remittances, urban agriculture, neighbours and relatives in the rural areas. Urban agriculture in Manzini, especially vegetable and maize cultivation and chicken-rearing for own consumption, has been a limited source of food for poor households, largely because it is not encouraged and supported by policymakers. This needs to change because it has considerable nutrition-boosting potential.

How have the poor in Manzini responded to food security challenges?

They have mitigated their insecure food situation by vigorously pursuing multiple innovative strategies that include sourcing food from friends and relatives in both rural and urban areas; buying cheaper food from informal food markets; borrowing food from neighbours; substituting micronutrient rich foods, such as meat and milk, with cheaper foods that are rich in starch; and reducing their number of meals from three to two a day.

In Swaziland, the national food security agenda has an evident rural bias with little attention given to the specific challenges of feeding the residents of urban areas. This needs to change because the locus of poverty is shifting to cities and most of the urban poor face food security challenges. The rural bias is characterized by a lack of systematic national and city strategies for reducing food insecurity among the urban poor in general and in informal settlements in particular. For example, the National Poverty Reduction Strategy and Action Programme of 2006 and other national action plans have a strong rural bias.

On the basis of these findings, several policy recommendations can be made to deal with food security challenges in the poor urban areas of Swaziland. It is vital for city and national policies that address urban food security to appreciate the complex relationship between household food security and a range of variables such as income, gender and household size. Also, there is an urgent need for government to target urban households specifically in addition to the focus on rural areas. A more national approach that covers both rural and urban areas will help Swaziland to move towards the achievement of the Millennium Development Goal to reduce hunger by 50%.

Clearly, city councils and national government need to support livelihood strategies pursued by the poor, such as urban agriculture, in order to help them to be more food secure. Also, there is a need for citywide policies that aim to strengthen targeted safety-net mechanisms for urban households that are food insecure. For example, the pro-poor food security policy that targets school children in urban areas should be broadened so that all children who are food insecure are assisted, but this requires a better targeting policy that ensures that all children from food-insecure households benefit from the programme. At the same time, government should create conditions that enable the informal food economy to flourish so that the urban poor can access cheaper and locally produced food.

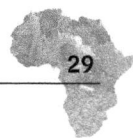

ENDNOTES

1   J. Crush and B. Frayne, *The Invisible Crisis: Urban Food Security in Southern Africa* AFSUN Series No. 1, Cape Town, 2010, p. 24.

2   FAO/WFP, Report on Crop and Food Supply Assessment Mission to Swaziland, July 2008; D. Tevera and J. Matondo. "Socio-Economic and Environmental Profile of Swaziland: An Introduction" In D. Tevera and J. Matondo, eds, *Socio-Economic Development and the Environment in Swaziland* (Kwaluseni: GEP, 2010), pp. 1-8; D. Tevera, "Migration and Development in Swaziland" *UNISWA Research Journal* 26(2011): 15-27.

3   FAO/WFP, "Report on Crop and Food Supply Assessment Mission to Swaziland" July 2008."

4   C. Asiedu, E. Asiedu and F. Owusu, "The Socio-Economic Determinants of HIV/AIDS Infection Rates in Lesotho, Malawi, Swaziland and Zimbabwe" *Development Policy Review* 30(3) (2012): 305-326; H. Yasmin, A. Salam, D. Manyatsi and O. Tagutanazvo. "The Socio-Economic Impact of HIV/AIDS in Swaziland" In Tevera and Matondo, eds, *Socio-Economic Development and the Environment in Swaziland*, pp. 325-42.

5   UNAIDS, *Country Factsheet: Swaziland* (Geneva, 2010).

6   R. Masuku, "HIV Prevalence and Associated Factors" In Central Statistical Office (CSO), *Swaziland Demographic and Health Survey 2006–07* (Mbabane, 2008), p. 221.

7   Ibid., p. 223.

8   Ibid., p. 225.

9   A. Whiteside, C. Andrade, L. Arrehag, S. Dlaminin, T. Ginindza and A. Parikh, "The Socio-Economic Impact of HIV/AIDS in Swaziland" Report for NERCHA and HEARD, 2006; A. Whiteside and F. Henry, "The Impact of HIV and AIDS Research: A Case Study from Swaziland" *Health Research Policy and Systems* 9(Suppl 1) (2011): S9; Yasmin et al, "Socio-Economic impact of HIV/AIDS in Swaziland."

10   S. Weiser, K. Leiter, D. Bangsberg, L. Butler, F. Percy-de Korte, Z. Hlanze, N. Phaladze, V. Iacopino and M. Heisler, "Food Insufficiency is Associated with High-Risk Sexual Behavior among Women in Botswana and Swaziland" *PLoS Medicine* 4(10) (2007): 1589-98; S. Naysmith, A. de Waal and A. Whiteside, "Revisiting New Variant Famine: The Case of Swaziland" *Food Security* 1(3) (2009): 251-60; M. Masuku and M. Sithole, "The Impact of HIV/AIDS on Food Security and Household Vulnerability in Swaziland" *Agrekon* 48(2) (2009): 200-22.

11   FAO/WFP, "Report on Crop and Food Supply Assessment Mission" p. 20.

12   Ibid.

13   M. Mabuza, S. Hendriks, G. Ortmann and M. Sithole, "The Impact of Food Aid on Maize Prices and Production in Swaziland" *Agrekon* 48(1) (2009): 85-105.

14   Swazi VAC, "Swaziland National Vulnerability Assessment"; A. Terry and M. Ryder, "Improving Food Security in Swaziland: The Transition from Subsistence to Communally Managed Cash Cropping" *Natural Resources Forum* 31(4) (2007): 263-72; O. Edje. "Drought and Food Security in Swaziland" In Tevera and

Matondo, *Socio-Economic Development and the Environment in Swaziland*, pp. 130-51; D. Dlamini and M. Masuku, "Land Tenure and Land Productivity: A Case of Maize Production in Swaziland" *Asian Journal of Agricultural Sciences* 3(4) (2011): 301-7; M. Mashinini, M. Sithole and M. Mabuza, "Contribution of Input Trade Fairs to Food Security in Rural Swaziland: Case Study of Households Under the Ngwempisi Constituency" *African Journal of Agricultural Research* 6(10) (2011): 2436-46; J. Vella, "Food and Water Security in Swaziland: Potential for Crises?" Strategic Analysis Paper, Future Directions International, 2012.

15   Swaziland National Vulnerability Assessment Committee (Swazi VAC), "Swaziland National Vulnerability Assessment September 2006" (Mbabane, 2006), p. 13.

16   Ibid., p. 25.

17   Ibid., p. 32.

18   N. Sikhosana, "Nutrition of Children and Adults" In CSO, *Swaziland Demographic and Health Survey 2006-07*, p. 143; S. Masuku-Maseko and E. Owage, "Child Malnutrition and Mortality in Swaziland: Situation analysis of the Immediate, Underlying and Basic Causes" *African Journal of Food, Agriculture, Nutrition and Development* 12(2) (2012): 5994-6006.

19   Sikhosana, "Nutrition of Children and Adults" pp. 161-2.

20   Swazi VAC and UNWFP, "Vulnerability and Food Insecurity in Urban Areas of Swaziland: An Assessment of the Impact of High Prices on Households in Four Regions" Mbabane, December 2008; T. Boudreau, "Livelihoods and Food Security Technical Assistance (LIFT): Swaziland Livelihood Data Analysis November, 2010" Pittsburgh, 2010.

21   Swazi VAC and UNWFP, "Vulnerability and Food Insecurity in Urban Areas" p. 22.

22   Ibid., pp. 22-24.

23   Ibid., p. 22.

24   M. Sihlongonyane, "Local Economic Development in Swaziland: The Case of Manzini City" *Urban Forum* 14(2-3) (2003): 244-63; D. Tevera and A. Zamberia. "Urbanization and Urban Management in Swaziland" In Tevera and Matondo, *Socio-Economic Development and the Environment in Swaziland*, pp. 272-88.

25   CSO, *Swaziland Demographic and Health Survey 2006-07*.

26   J. Crush and B. Frayne, "Supermarket Expansion and the Informal Food Economy in Southern African Cities: Implications for Urban Food Security" *Journal of Southern African Studies* 37(2011): 781-807.

27   M. Miles, "Women's Groups and Urban Poverty: The Swaziland Experience" In A. Tostensen, I. Tvedten and M. Vaa, eds, *Associational Life in African Cities: Popular Responses to the Urban Crisis* (Stockholm: Nordika Afrikainstitutet, 2001), pp. 64-73; S. Dlamini, "The Role of the Local Authority in Accommodating Street Trading: The Case of Manzini City Council in Swaziland" MSc Thesis, University of Natal, Durban, 2002.

28   J. Crush, A. Hovorka and D. Tevera, "Food Security in Southern African Cities: The Place of Urban Agriculture" *Progress in Development Studies* 11(2011): 285-305

29   B. Masina, "Planning the Growth of Peri-Urban Settlements: Case Study of Manzini in Swaziland" MSc Thesis, International Institute for Geo-Information Science and Earth Observation, University of Twente, 2003.

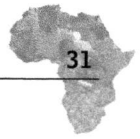

30   B. Frayne, "Pathways of Food: Migration and Food Security in Southern African
      Cities" *International Development Planning Review* 32 (2010): 83-104; J. Crush,
      Migration, Development and Urban Food Security AFSUN Series No. 9, Cape Town,
      2012.

31   M. Masarirambi, N. Mhazo, A. Dlamini and A. Mutukumira, "Common
      Indigenous Fermented Foods and Beverages Produced in Swaziland: A Review"
      Journal of Food Science and Technology 46(6) (2009): 505-8; M. Masarirambi, V.
      Mavuso, V. Sonwe, T. Nkambule and N. Mhazo, "Indigenous Post-Harvest
      Handling and Processing of Traditional Vegetables in Swaziland: A Review"
      African Journal of Agricultural Research 5(24) (2010): 3333-41.

32   J. Coates, A. Swindale and P. Bilinsky, "Household Food Insecurity Access Scale
      (HFIAS) for Measurement of Food Access: Indicator Guide (Version 3)" Food and
      Nutrition Technical Assistance Project, Academy for Educational Development,
      Washington, D.C., 2007, p.18.

33   Ibid., pp. 21-2.

34   A. Swindale and P. Bilinsky, "Household Dietary Diversity Score (HDDS) for
      measurement of Household Food Access: Indicator Guide (Version 2)" Food and
      Nutrition Technical Assistance Project, Academy for Educational Development,
      Washington, D.C., 2006.

35   P. Bilinsky and A. Swindale, "Months of Adequate Household Food Provisioning
      (MAHFP) for Measurement of Household Food Access: Indicator Guide"
      Food and Nutrition Technical Assistance Project, Academy for Educational
      Development, Washington, D.C., 2007.

36   G. Tawodzera, L. Zanamwe and J. Crush, *The State of Food Insecurity in Harare,
      Zimbabwe* AFSUN Paper No. 13, Cape Town, 2012.

37   African Economic Outlook, "Swaziland" at http://www.africaneconomicoutlook.
      org/en/countries/southern-africa/swaziland/

38   Swazi VAC and UNWFP, "Vulnerability and Food Insecurity in Urban Areas of
      Swaziland."

39   Dlamini and Masuku, "Land Tenure and Land Productivity" p. 304.

40   M. Masuku, "An Analysis of the Broiler Supply Chain in Swaziland: A Case Study
      of the Manzini Region" *Asian Journal of Agricultural Sciences* 3(6) (2011): 492-9.

41   W. Pendleton, N. Nickanor and A. Pomuti, *The State of Food Insecurity in Windhoek,
      Namibia* AFSUN Series No. 14, Cape Town, 2012.